TABLE DECORATING

CLB 4299
Published originally under the title "Der Tisch Schön Gedeckt".
by Gräfe und Unzer Verlag GmbH, München
© 1993 by Gräfe und Unzer Verlag GmbH, München
This edition published 1995 by
Tiger Books International PLC, Twickenham
English-language translation copyright
© 1995 CLB Publishing, Godalming, Surrey
All rights reserved
Printed and bound in Italy by New Interlitho
ISBN 1-85501-624-9

TABLE DECORATING

BEATE RABE

TIGER BOOKS INTERNATIONAL
LONDON

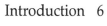

Contents

"Then, at the invitation of the hostess, the company made towards the decorated, round dining room, from which the festive scent of flowers and a cool breeze wafted, whetting the appetites of the entrants. We seated ourselves at the skilfully planned places ... and so eleven of us made a colourful group around the table, the lower end of which was bare. From the centre of the table rose two huge porcelain figures with painted faces, holding large bowls heaped with fresh fruit and flowers above their heads. The other things which were on the table or which gradually followed seemed to announce an extended feast. Fine wines, from the deepest purple-red to the yellowy white wine, whose lively foam caps the second half of any feast, gleamed now from the table between the bowls and platters, now from the serving table in the background."

This is what Mozart experienced on his journey to Prague as a surprise guest at a wedding breakfast. A contemporary of Mozart recounts this episode and describes in fitting words the celebratory atmosphere, the invitingly laid-out rooms, the famous guests and the enjoyable conversation. It was so pleasant that what had been intended to be a brief pause turned into a glittering party where lots of interesting new friendships were made.

In his story, Mozart's contemporary describes the essential components of such events. A festive meal does not just depend on an enticing menu and fine wines. A carefully considered seating plan, a pleasant atmosphere and, last but not least, a splendid table setting are just as important.

This book will show, using plentiful illustrations, what Mozart's colleague describes with such admiration, not on quite such a splendid scale perhaps, but individual and varied, nevertheless. The table settings given here and the ideas behind them are not intended to amaze you but rather to make you want to try them. They should inspire you to have a go at flexing your creative muscles, not to build an artistic still life.

Your efforts (and ours) will be well worth it when, the next time – as you expectantly await your guests' comments on a new and unusual table decoration – they say excitedly, "Now that's really something special!"

This miniature furniture forms part of the decorations for the house-moving brunch (page 66).

It's bound to happen sooner or later: you're expecting guests, whether just a few or a large number, informally or to celebrate a special occasion, on the spur of the moment or formally invited. Then it will be all hands to the pump for the preparations.

Some hostesses have to spend a lot of time thinking and planning in advance so that everything is taken care of; others cope with the preparations as they go along. Of course, everyone experiences the odd doubt as to whether the celebration will be a success. However, it doesn't matter which category of hostess you come under; spending a little time thinking about the preparations will always help contribute to the success of a meal.

A good idea is often the starting point for success, and it's always the same with ideas – sometimes they appear straight away, at other times you have to work hard at them. Experience shows, however, that it is worth the effort.

Perhaps the time of year will provide you with a theme or a definite opportunity. Perhaps a hobby of one of your guests will set you thinking along the right lines, or you will relate to a common experience, or perhaps you will leaf through this book and be inspired by one of the table settings shown here.

In addition to a good start you need one other thing – consistency. Hard work at the start is only worth it if your guests also notice it. For this reason everything should match the original theme as closely as possible. Consistency means that sometimes everyday things can be put together in a completely different way. For example, sometimes a nice new vase will have to stay in the cupboard because unfortunately, this time, it doesn't fit in with the scheme. Sometimes it means saying goodbye to your usual tablecloth or flower arrangement. Instead you may find yourself putting wide silk ribbons on the table, or colourful autumn leaves.

There is one thing that you must remember, however; that everything should relate in some way to you and your guests. No matter how clever your creation, if it has been put together just for the sake of it, it will fall flat. The spark of excitement won't be there, and all your hard work will be dismissed with "Oh yes, very nice." What a shame.

For this reason the table settings in this book are intended to inspire you to create your own personal decorative ideas. They are not intended as a recipe for instant success.

It is much nicer if you let the table and room decorations speak for you, and what interests you, or let them speak for your guests, the guest of honour, or the occasion which has brought everyone together. They can also express the things you and your guests have experienced together, or things you would like to discuss with them.

Symbolic decorations can speak louder to your guests than any number of words. Turn a lovingly arranged decoration into a pictorial eulogy for your guest of honour, especially if he or she is not too keen on table talk.

Decorations can be an important ice-breaker, especially if your guests don't know each other. Thoughtful and eye-catching displays can initiate conversation.

They can also revive traditional celebrations and liven up the proceedings. Just when guests have got used to the same old things, an unusual and fitting alternative may provide a pleasant surprise.

Whenever your table decorations express a clever and interesting idea, combined with effective, well-thought-out details, your guests will be fired with enthusiasm and will see this as a sign of your attentiveness, as a gift from you to them. It's all up to you.

Colours – spoilt for choice

Your choice of colour will determine the style and ambience of a table, so don't rely on a quick decision. Colours can be used quite consciously to achieve precisely the effect you are hoping for.

It may help you to run through the colour palette, starting with the colour which appears on almost every table – green.

Green for freshness

For nature lovers, the fresh green of flowers and leaves brings life into the house, especially during the winter months. Therefore green is a welcome addition to the table, because besides its fresh appearance, it has another quality. Green lifts and emphasises other colours, especially its complementary colour, red. You can exploit this characteristic if you place big green leaves on the table and then

lay a single, or just a few, brightly coloured blossoms on top (for example, rhododendrons or hydrangeas).

However, layering shades of green can also have a very stimulating effect. Simply use green throughout – green tablecloth, napkins, decorative ribbons, green crockery and green candles for a feast of freshness.

Classic grey

To many people grey isn't a colour at all but a state of mind: sad, cold and clinical. The same applies here as elsewhere – it depends what you do with it! In architecture and interior design, grey provides a neutral backdrop against which other colours provide intentional accents. Apply the same principle to your table. Grey is neutral and can be combined with warm or cold colours. A grey tablecloth is an ideal ground on which to give a wide range of colours full play.

If you like cool colours, you can bring together the grey ground with chrome or steel, mirrored glass or silver, thus emphasising a hi-tech atmosphere or one of cold splendour, both of which can result in a classic effect. Depending on the lighting, such a table setting can cause an interesting play of light and reflections.

You can create a warmer and more tasteful atmosphere using a combination of warm colours and grey, with a high proportion of red or yellow. Candlelight can make a great difference if you are trying to warm up the overall effect of a grey scheme.

White – simple or celebratory

Like grey, white can express a wide range of moods. White achieves a different effect depending on the colour with which it is combined. A white table setting can look cool and simple, but it can also look classic and elegant.

A summery table dressed with marguerites, daisies and white tulle, on the contrary, gives an attractive impression of frivolity and relaxation. White combined with pastels and lots of silver makes for a festive table design. You can imitate a festive wedding breakfast with white table linen and crockery, big silver candlesticks and lavish champagne-coloured floral arrangements.

Yellow – bright and cheerful

Yellow is associated with sunshine, light, vitality and cheerfulness; and the many yellow spring flowers, such as narcissus, tulips and primroses, herald summer. Yellow is found throughout the whole year, however, with wonderful sunflowers in late summer and the golden yellow of leaves in autumn. Thus it is almost always possible for you to have yellow on the table, the cheerful effect being emphasised by further yellow table accoutrements. Napkins tied with yellow ribbons and candles in various shades of the same colour are just two of the options.

Red for fiery warmth

Red is the boldest and most impulsive of colours; brilliant red conveys warmth and excitement at the same time; red roses are the symbol of romanticism, passion and beauty. Red is always dominant and striking, and for this reason can sometimes be a little oppressive. You should use red with a certain amount of restraint when it comes to your table decorations. Combined with shades of pale pink, red conveys warmth and sensuality; when combined with grey and green, the fiery qualities of red are emphasised. Red can be warm and cosy, as when it is associated with Christmas; or traditional and classic, as illustrated. A lot depends on the lighting in each case, so if you are decorating with red, you should pay particular attention to the lighting in the dining room. Just try out a few different lighting options so that you bring out the tones in the colour as you imagine them. Direct a spotlight onto the centre of the table, provide the table with indirect lighting, make a chain of lights, or light candles. The colour combinations will be different every time.

Blue creates a tasteful atmosphere

From the palest dove grey via powerful steel blue to deepest midnight blue, a wide range of shades can be used for decoration. Sometimes blue can be cool, making you think of darkness and shade; sometimes it can be invigorating and provide inspiration for many different creations. Blue also works well in combination with other colours. The fact that it harmonises so well creates an in-depth effect and a tasteful atmosphere around the table. The classic contrasting combination of blue and white captivates with its clarity and energy, whilst the lesser contrast between blue and green can on the other hand create a very stylish ambience.

Pastel colours radiate gentle elegance

Pink, lilac, salmon, cream and champagne are a contrast to the glowing primary colours. Despite their delicate colouring effect, they are neither pale nor unobtrusive and can be very elegant when combined with white. Soft contrasting tones help to create a peaceful, gentle atmosphere. If they are combined with colourful crockery, the effect is more disruptive; so pastel tones should be linked with white china and vases, enhanced by glass and silver. For example, a large silver or glass bowl filled with water, with pastel-coloured roses floating on the surface, is very effective. Obviously such colours are less suitable for use at rustic picnics or lively parties.

Two paths to successful colour selection

The choice is yours: do you want your table to reflect harmonious shades, or to be more striking and impulsive? If you want to achieve the first effect, a harmonious overall picture, choose a base colour for the design (if this is not already determined by the crockery or surroundings). Everything else which is added to the table should closely follow this basic colour.

The alternative, the eye-catching table, is based on contrasts, and possibly unconventional colour combinations. An unusual colour scheme can be created by different variations of complementary colours (such as red and green, blue and orange, yellow and purple). If you make strong contrasts between dark and light you are sure to achieve an effect that your guests will notice.

The history of crockery is a chequered one. There were times when nobles and merchants tried to outdo each other with beautiful china. In fact the splendour on the table was more important than the food on the plates. The finest porcelain (known as white gold) was painted with in several layers and decorated with gold leaf. Simplicity was the last thing anyone had in mind.

More recent times have provided us with cheap paper and plastic crockery. It didn't matter whether it looked good or not – the most important thing was that it was practical. Decorated and disposable items are all crockery, but there is a world of difference between them.

It is easy to see how stylish and colourful they can be, and how many different shapes and types of materials are now available. All you have to do is look in the window of a department store, or take a look at the pages of this book. There is elegant white crockery with the traditional gold edging, rustic pottery, romantic designs in pale colours or bolder ones with a gaudy mix of colours. Every type of decoration creates a different impression, sometimes powerful, sometimes more restrained. Use the effect which your crockery creates to bring about your decorative ideas, and you are already halfway to a successful table decoration.

There is an enormous range of white crockery, from canteen standard to that stamped "by appointment to". The range of uses for white china is just as numerous because white crockery is restrained but also full of character. It combines cool sophistication with relaxed informality. You must use your other decorations to set the tone. Underplates in coloured china or silver will make a strong statement by either introducing colour or lending an air of refinement to your table.

Is your crockery striking? Of an unusual colour, pattern or design? Then make use of these colours and shapes in your additional decorations. The tablecloth should be a strong colour, with the decorative elements appearing again as little touches in the centre of the table; gaudy crockery should be brightly lit; the floral decoration on the table should match the floral pattern on the crockery. Think of ways in which the crockery and other decorations can be combined rather than just standing them next to one another on the table without any apparent connection.

Earthenware crockery with natural-coloured glazes and pottery creates a predominantly rustic effect. You can emphasise this by using natural materials for decoration, such as a tablecloth of coarse linen or sisal, clay pots as flower vases, thick ropes as napkin rings, and serving utensils made of wood; together with wild flowers, moss and grasses. Next time you have the chance, you should prove that these things can easily be combined in a tasteful table setting!

There is always the chance that you won't have enough crockery for a large number of guests, so you must learn to improvise skilfully. The more bravely you face up to it, the more successful you are likely to be. Combine your dinner service with glass plates, or extend a colourful china service with plain white, or vice versa. However, whatever you use, the style should be similar to that of your main service, rather than mixing fine bone china with rustic "farmhouse" crockery.

Glasses – clearly stylish

This invention is older even than the ancient Romans, who prized the product of melting sand, limestone and soda, and the attractive shapes and practical containers which could be made from this refined material.

Glass is found today in almost all walks of life, and it is hard to imagine life without it. The range of drinking vessels extends nowadays from cheap moulded glass to hand-blown, engraved designer glasses.

The differences in quality depend on the composition of the glass as well as on the way in which it is produced. The use of different raw materials and the melting process are decisive in determining the quality of the glass. Good-quality glasses are usually hand-blown, the sides are engraved and they don't have a seam. On the other hand, moulded glasses are rarely as clear as hand-made ones, they have a small bulge at the rim and usually have a seam on the stem or foot. However, they are much cheaper than blown glass, and therefore much more practical for many uses.

Machine-blown glasses, which are currently widely available, offer good quality with the advantages of blown glass but at a price which means you can buy different glasses to suit different occasions.

The number of different shapes can be puzzling, and the already confusing range is constantly being expanded by new creations. However, some shapes have become "classics" for certain drinks.

Here are a few examples to help you serve your guests their drink in the right type of glass.

Brandy   *Port*   *Claret*   *Water*

Fruit juices, lemonade and mineral water can all be served in highball glasses, although you can also get water glasses, which are usually between a white wine and a red wine glass in size, in most wine-glass designs. For red wine, a bellied glass with a fairly large capacity is typical, so that the wine's bouquet has room to develop, because your sense of smell is just as important as your tastebuds when drinking wine. White wine is served chilled in smaller glasses. The smaller size means that the glasses must be topped up more often so the wine is always fresh and cool. Narrow, elegant "flutes" are better for sparkling wines and champagne than shallow champagne saucers, because if they are served in the latter type of glass the carbon dioxide quickly escapes and the pleasurable sparkling sensation is lost. There are too many different glasses for aperitifs and digestifs to be explained here, but the illustration below shows a brandy balloon, a port glass and a sherry copita. Together with the others they provide a basic range of glasses.

White wine   *Dessert wine*   *Beer*   *Sherry*   *Champagne*

Should it be stainless steel or chrome, plastic or wood, silver or gold? Lavishly decorated or simple, classic or avant-garde in design? Should oyster forks or a cake slice be included? Should there be six place settings or twelve? For many people the choice of their cutlery is one of the most difficult (but most pleasurable) household decisions. However, your choice should be guided by one thing: cutlery is a tool and not an exhibition piece. An old silver service which clearly shows the signs of many years' use is much nicer than a well-preserved collection of cutlery which is only used on very special occasions. There is a further principle which you should apply when choosing your cutlery: the cutlery must be suited to the job for which it is intended, it should not be impractical. Good designers work according to the tried and tested principle of "form follows function"; i.e., it is only a good design when it works perfectly. This shouldn't prevent you, however, from considering interesting, unusual cutlery works of art as collectors' items; but for eating, they must be practical. When it comes to choosing the material, in addition to the price (depending on the size of the collection, sterling silver cutlery is a real investor's item), a further argument must be taken into consideration. From time to time silver has to be cleaned. On the other hand stainless steel cutlery is much easier to care for, and at the same time, if it is good quality, the surface is much harder and less likely to suffer from scratches and the signs of wear and tear. However, manufacturers of solid silver cutlery generally offer a longer after-sales guarantee than manufacturers of stainless steel cutlery. If you don't want to buy everything at once, then the guarantee on offer can also help you to reach your decision. All these considerations, which you

should bear in mind, don't make the choice any easier. Therefore you should take the time to select the cutlery which best suits you. Obviously you can start with the basic equipment and gradually add the more unusual items – as gifts from relatives, for example. However, the extensive range available can be confusing.

There are many cutlery manufacturers, and there is a tool to suit every occasion at the table. You can choose a good selection of useful cutlery from the multiplicity of shapes, to suit your requirements.

The examples shown here can be considered as a basic cutlery service and may be used as the inspiration for your own personal service. Of course, you can always expand the range to suit yourself.

In addition the combination of different types of cutlery, especially serving utensils, can introduce a welcome change to the table. In this way cutlery which has been passed down through the family, but which has suffered with the years, can be given new life when combined with more modern cutlery. You can emphasise the combination of old and new if old cutlery is decorated with a monogram or crest. In specialist cutlery shops you may well be able to find an expert who would be able to engrave the traditional symbol on new cutlery. In this way, both old and new will bear your mark.

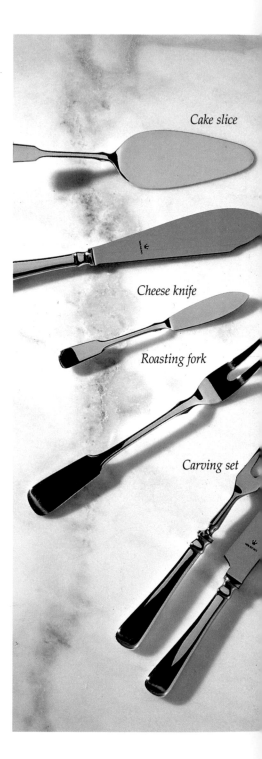

Cake slice

Cheese knife

Roasting fork

Carving set

Soup ladle

Butter knife

Fish knife and fork

Fish servers

Asparagus slice

y ladle

Salad servers

Tablecloths – a fashion parade for your table

Thoughts of an attractive table setting usually start with a freshly laundered tablecloth which is carefully spread over the table. Sometimes that's as far as the table decorations get – which is a shame, because with a few tucks and a bit of imagination, just a tablecloth on its own can provide your table with an effective "outfit".

There are a few basic rules which will help you to make the most of your tablecloth.

The tablecloth must fit the table.

This makes sense, because nothing is more detrimental to the effect of a table than a cloth which is too small. On the other hand, your guests won't enjoy fighting to disentangle their legs from acres of cloth hanging down from the table. It should still be possible to sit comfortably at a fully clothed table.

The tablecloth must match the crockery.

A white tablecloth provides a perfect background for table design. The crockery or other decorative items can then add highlights. Coloured or patterned cloths must be a good match with the crockery – either with harmonising colours and patterns or as a planned contrast, but match it must.

The tablecloth must suit the occasion.

A celebratory table can be very effective when dressed with gleaming taffeta or moiré fabrics. Rustic decorations are strengthened by coarse linen or hessian tablecloths. Gentle pastel tones emphasise thoughtful occasions, whereas you can cheerfully use lots of colours and contrasting patterns in the tablecloth for happy celebrations.

The tablecloth must suit the surroundings.

Avoid clashes of style! Your guests don't just see the table; they also see the surroundings – the furniture, the walls, the fabrics and pictures. Particularly daring attempts at table decoration with paper, paint or foil instead of a cloth may well be very effective, but they must suit the ambience in the room, otherwise they seem artificial.

And finally – the tablecloth must suit you.

Additional tips on tablecloth use:

For an elegant table you should hide the sharp edges of the table under the tablecloth. Cover the table with quilting, which encloses the edge of the table (you can possibly use a sewn-in elastic border). Sharp edges are then a thing of the past and your table is more streamlined.

You can easily give a buffet table a little extra height by building up different levels on the table with cardboard boxes, and then spreading the tablecloth over them. It's quick and easy to do, looks good, and at the same time makes the buffet treats much easier for your guests to see.

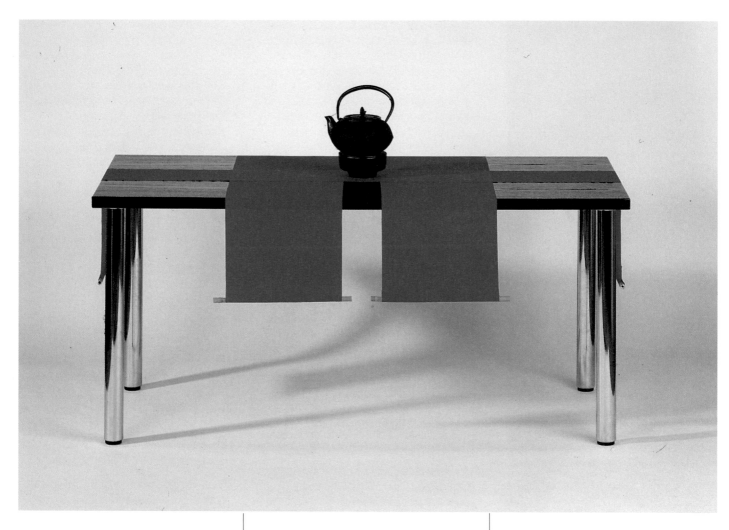

Give your tablecloth its marching orders! If you want to treat your guests to a banquet from the Far East, simply use crêpe paper instead and place it in strong geometric designs on the table. The ends are stiffened with lengths of cane, which emphasise the impression of the East. If crêpe paper seems too simple to you, lengths of fabric or genuine Japanese paper will achieve the same effect. This type of decoration can also be used very effectively on a low coffee table. For once you can bring your guests to their knees without a qualm! Then let the exotic charm of Far Eastern culture shine through in your other decorations – in the flower arrangements, for example, where fans of ikebana will be able to really give full reign to their skills.

Would you like to show off the lovely wooden or glass-topped table in your house? Then don't hide it under a tablecloth! Drape a piece of cloth over the table like a scarf, or arrange it in the centre of the table. It will create a good spot of colour which will emphasise the natural effect of your table. If you want to have several dashes of colour and use the contrasts to heighten the effect of the table decorations, then you can spread several different coloured lengths of fabric over the table, either side by side or interwoven.

Gathered like a summer dress

This little trick is quick to do, but none the less striking, especially for long tables with a deep fall of tablecloth. Gather the cloth in the centre and secure the gathers with a safety pin. Then, depending on the time of year and the occasion, you can fasten on green leaves or flowers, a big bow or a decorative ball. A tablecloth gathered in this way is particularly suited to a buffet table.

If you want to dress a very long buffet table or a large round table in this way, gather the overhanging cloth evenly in several places and secure in the same way as before. The resulting festoons recall celebration tables from the Baroque era.

Adorned like a bride

Do you like tulle? If so, then take a long strip of it and fasten it around the table in loops to make a garland. Secure the tulle to the tablecloth at several points, either with safety pins or by tacking the two fabrics together. You should ensure that the colours in the tulle and the tablecloth go together. The effect becomes really special if you fasten ivy or flowers at the points where the garland is secured.

If you haven't got enough tulle to make a garland, as an alternative you can use smaller pieces to make big bows which can then be attached to the sides of the tablecloth.

You can achieve a more breezy and informal effect by using lots of brightly coloured tulle bows, including a few neon colours, fastened at random across the cloth. However, don't go mad; too many bows and garish colours are more likely to annoy your guests than interest them.

The art of place settings

Have you ever watched the precise and practised way in which professionals in a good hotel or restaurant set a big table for a five- or six-course meal? Lots of different glasses and table silver are placed in exactly the right spot without hesitation. The number of items involved in a setting may seem confusing to you.

However, there is a clear rule for everything.

Guests start with the cutlery furthest away from the plate and work inwards during the course of the meal. The same procedure applies to glasses. The drink which is served first is put into the glass which is furthest from the centre of the plate. There is often also a side plate, which is placed to the left of the setting.

These few rules are so basic and clear that they can become a matter of routine for any guest, so you no longer have to worry about which knife, fork or spoon to use next during the meal.

For the preparations to be as straightforward for you, you should be clear in your mind before setting the table about which courses are going to be served during the meal, and which drinks will accompany them. Then the cutlery is laid out in reverse order – in other words the cutlery for the last course is closest to the plate and for the first course on the outside, furthest away from the plate.

Here are two further tips to ensure your place settings are perfect every time.

Apply the "rule of thumb"! There should be a gap of a thumb's width between the edge of the plate and the cutlery, and between the cutlery handles and the edge of the table.

Try to avoid a game of hide and seek. The cutlery should not be hidden under the edge of the plate. Your guests would far rather have what they need to hand straight away than have to go hunting for it.

The illustrations on the following two pages show two place settings for meals with only a few courses, which will probably cover most meals which you cook at home. Two other examples illustrate variations on more complex settings for four-course meals.

Crockery: a dinner plate is laid ready for the main course. The dessert plate or dish is not laid.

Cutlery: the fork and knife are set ready for the main course; the dessert spoon is placed, with the handle to the right, above the plate.

Glasses: if you are serving wine, the appropriate red or white wine glass should stand above the knife, to the right. Beer glasses or other glasses should be put in the same place.

Crockery: a deep plate has been put ready for an Italian pasta dish. The dinner plate underneath serves as a place plate. For Italian meals you must have a side plate for bread.

Cutlery: for the pasta the spoon and fork are placed to the right and left of the plate respectively, the dessert spoon – with the handle to the right – above the plate, and the butter knife on the side plate.

Glasses: water is a must. A water glass is there ready for mineral water, with the wine glass placed to the left and above the water glass.

Crockery: the dinner plate and soup cup are placed on top of a place plate. In many cases the soup is served straight into the cups, rather than from a tureen, so at first only the soup cup saucers are set.

Cutlery: the soup spoon is placed on the outside right, followed by the knife and fork for the starter. The knife and fork for the main course go on the inside of these, with the dessert spoon above the plate.

Glasses: a white wine glass is positioned to the right, just above the soup spoon. To the left and above this is the water glass, which is used frequently. The red wine glass for the main course is placed on the same line, above the water glass.

Crockery: a soup plate and dinner plate stand on a place plate in the centre. A side plate is placed to the left, a little above the forks.

Cutlery: the soup spoon is laid on the right, next to the fish knife. The fish fork is on the outside left. The knife and fork for the main course are inside the fish service. A small butter knife or starter knife is placed on the side plate. The dessert service is placed above the plate, the fork nearest the plate with the handle to the left, and the spoon above it with the handle to the right.

Glasses: the glasses are placed on the right, above the soup spoon. Starting from immediately above the spoon they are a white wine glass for the starter, a water glass, and a red wine glass for the main course.

Table napkins – the art of folding

Napkins belong on every attractive table setting, not just because of their intended use, but also as an eye-catching decoration.

In Baroque times, napkin folding was regarded as an art. The artists created stylised flowers, birds and fantastic creatures for each guest. Even if such time-consuming work would be a bit over the top for our decorations, napkins can still be used effectively for decorative purposes.

You should practise new folding techniques on a piece of paper. For folds to work, the napkin will need to be starched before ironing – otherwise the shape won't be rigid enough, no matter how good your folding technique.

Would you rather use paper serviettes for a particular occasion? Then try folding simpler shapes, because paper is relatively stiff. There is an ever increasing range of paper serviettes available, with all kinds of different colours and patterns, to provide inspiration for your table-setting ideas.

The fan

1. Fold the napkin in half, then fold half of the rectangle into concertina folds.

2. Pinch the concertina folds together, and fold the whole thing over in the middle so that the long edges are together.

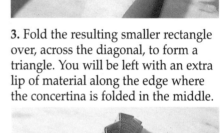

3. Fold the resulting smaller rectangle over, across the diagonal, to form a triangle. You will be left with an extra lip of material along the edge where the concertina is folded in the middle.

4. Fold this back on itself to form a stand, then open up the folds of the fan.

Three waves

1. Fold the napkin in three to form a long rectangle.

2. Take each end of the rectangle and fold in halfway towards the middle. Then take the folded ends and fold these into the middle.

3. You should end up with a square. This forms the first two waves.

4. You get the third wave if you fold the square in backwards on itself a little, so that the waves lie in layers on top of each other.

Table napkins – the art of folding

Butterfly

1. Fold in the top and bottom edges of the napkin so that they meet in the middle.

2. Now fold the napkin in half, placing the folded-in sides on top of each other, to form a long rectangle.

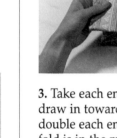

3. Take each end of the rectangle and draw in towards the centre, then double each end back on itself so the fold is in the middle of the rectangle and the loose end on the outside.

4. Then on one side draw the upper fold from the outside to the middle and crease the resulting triangle in the middle to make a double fold.

5. If you repeat the procedure on the other side, you will have shaped the butterfly's wings.

Boat

1. Fold the napkin in four, then – working from the loose ends – fold over to form a triangle.

3. Tuck the remaining points in underneath.

4. Fold the triangle together lengthways so that both points are on the inside.

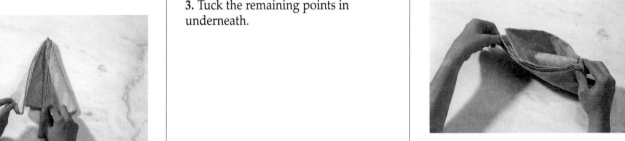

5. If you hold the shape tightly on the short side, and gently pull the folds up one after the other at the pointed end, you will end up with a napkin "boat".

2. Turn it over so that the four loose corners are underneath, then fold the two corners in to the middle towards you.

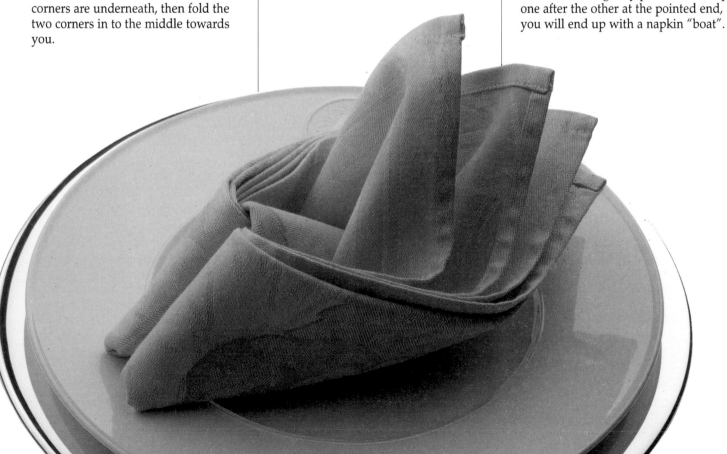

A few tips to help you with design:

Menu cards should be an honest indication of what your guests can expect. You can be as creative as you like in the choice of dishes, but don't blow your own trumpet too much, because you will have to deliver the goods. The format of the cards shouldn't overpower the other decorations, and remember that your guests may want to keep the card by the side of their place during the meal. If you want to use a large sheet of paper, then tie it up with a pretty ribbon; menu "scrolls" are a good alternative to cards.

For big celebrations – for example, wedding breakfasts – a hand-written menu card is often too time consuming. Why not contact a small printer with your menu details and let them print the cards to a design that you like?

If you are celebrating in a restaurant or hotel, then you should use the menu cards provided by their hospitality service. Be prepared to listen to their advice, but do make sure you have some influence on the choice of design.

Both examples shown here give you an idea of how to list on the menu card all the delicacies which you intend to serve your guests.

What are you having to drink? Either list the drinks details after the dessert, or coffee – or if you are using a folded card, they should be written on the inside leaf, on the left. If you are serving a beverage to match every course, the drinks should be listed on the left in the order which matches the courses listed on the right.

It goes without saying that you will be offering mineral water and other refreshing drinks, so these don't have to be included on the menu.

It has become normal to expect that menu cards and seating plans are purely a matter of etiquette and reserved for official occasions, as they are thought more than a little excessive for a private dinner party. It would be a pity if this idea were to persist, because menu cards for a small dinner party or place cards for a tea party in your home can be a gesture which brings people closer together and, if you do it properly, a sign that you are in command of your role as a hostess. They also make an eye-catching part of the overall table decorations.

Imaginatively designed menu cards lead to anticipation of a delicious meal and afterwards your guests can take them home as an attractive memento.

Menu cards can be real works of art; but for your personal use they don't have to be, because even a little careful, well-thought-out decoration can lend the cards a very appealing and personal air. Use photographs or silhouettes, satin or cord ribbons, flowers, leaves or other materials which suit the theme. The photograph on the facing page shows several examples which appear on various tables throughout this book.

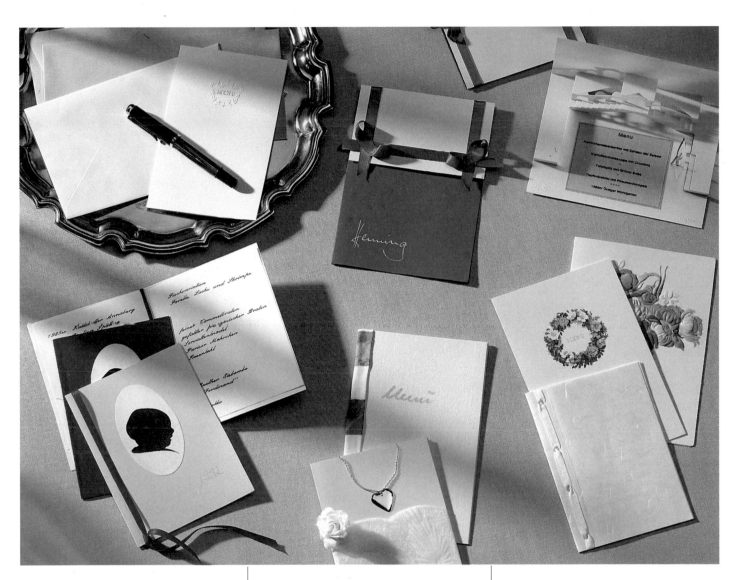

What about the seating plan?

If you don't want to leave anything to chance, you can use decorative place cards as a friendly guide to seating, in order to bring together the guests who ought to get to know each other. Every woman should have a suitable man at her side, and couples and possible cliques should be separated for a few hours.

Let your guests find out who's sitting where by themselves, or make it into a little game so that table partners get to know each other easily before sitting down. The first rule of seating plans is that the men sit on the left of the women. Banqueting specialists observe a whole host of other rules for special occasions which need not concern you for dinner parties at home. If you follow your intuition, you are bound to get most of it right.

Tip:

If you are using both menu cards and place cards, you should avoid using different styles. Both types of paper, colour and decoration should match, providing a uniform picture.

The table illustrated here is not just a still life; it is a compilation of a small selection of things which are used as decorations for various tables in this book. This should give you a few ideas about the many accessories which surround you in your house.

Every container, every sculpture, pretty stones or shells, decorative ribbons or marbles can provide you with ideas for table decorations. Don't be afraid to use simple, everyday items from house and garden, or even foodstuffs. What about wire, pieces of cloth, sand, old pots or flasks, balls, candles, mirrors or even toy cars? What is wrong with a large cabbage or asparagus as a replacement for, or addition to, flowers? Why not use fifty sharpened pencils for an accountant's fiftieth birthday party table? Or why not put brown leaves on the table, when we enjoy them so much outdoors in autumn?

But you can be inspired by other things, which don't have to be commonplace – such as the wide range of lights, vases, napkin rings and knife rests in specialist shops. Many accessories that you will find there will provide you with inspiration for eye-catching additions to your table.

Next comes the bouquet!

Flowers have always played an important role in table decorations, which is just as it should be, because their natural beauty, their fresh smell and sometimes their symbolic meanings are with us throughout our lives.

Even if you don't have the skills of a florist, it can often make an enjoyable change if you don't buy a prepared bouquet. You can make wonderful individual creations using a few blooms or flowers from the garden, when leaves, grasses and branches, and your imagination, will give inspiration to your efforts.

You must ensure, however, that bouquets of flowers retain their natural charm. You should not subject these beautiful products of nature to artificial ingredients and alien arrangements. A colourful posy of wild flowers is very effective in a simple vase made of natural materials or in a wooden box (with a waterproof lining, of course). A bunch of sunflowers looks great with rustic clay colours. You can happily scatter spring flowers across the table and there are more than enough flowers which will look their best in your favourite vases.

Tip:

When choosing your decorative materials, originality is the key and you shouldn't lose sight of this in garish, expensive materials. The examples illustrated on the following pages show that you don't have to rely on expensive materials which are damaging to the environment when buying materials and designing your table decorations. Natural materials offer bountiful inspiration for interesting table design.

A journey through the year

Spring, with its fresh colours, the magnificent blooms of summer, autumnal woods and wintry mountains and streams – all these seasons have been the subject of many songs and paintings.

You can also capture these moods on your table. A few examples which cover the whole year show you how to do this. It doesn't matter when, and which occasion, you are celebrating. Such tables create an unmistakeable atmosphere.

The birth of spring

It's here

*Spring flutters its blue ribbon through the
skies once more;*
*sweet, familiar scents drift like harbingers
across the land.*
*Violets are already dreaming, making their
appearance soon.*
Hark, from afar the faint music of a harp!
Spring, you're here!
I heard you!
(A poem by Eduard Mörike)

Have you heard spring? Don't delay,
bring it inside.

What to do:

The yellow of a tablecloth, place plates
and flowers combined with a white
lace cloth and white china provide the
refeshing background colour for the
table, symbolising the tenderness of
the new buds.

The flower garlands on the place
plates contain violets, forget-me-nots
and ranunculus fastened onto a
twisted wire. With a little skill you
will be able to make the garlands
yourself. You should keep the
garlands in water until the start of the
meal so that the flowers retain their
freshness and colour. Any individual
blooms which are left over from
making the garlands can then simply
be scattered across the table.

The blue ribbon which is fastened in a
bow at the end of the garland and
which is wound loosely across the
table is a symbolic interpretation of
Mörike's poem.

Simple white linen napkins fit in
with the theme here; they are held
like flowers in round, silver
napkin rings.

Tip:

If you want to re-create the birth of
spring in a more naturalistic and rustic
way, then place small clay pots with
crocuses, narcissii, primroses or tulips
on the table. Continue the theme with
flower bulbs spread across the table as
well as fresh grass or twigs with
delicate green leaves. You can use
butterflies or birds folded out of paper
for place cards.

For many people a country walk at Easter is a good old tradition. It gets you out into the country and you are able to enjoy the fact that spring has arrived to the full. Also, Easter is a traditional time for visiting; relatives or friends come to stay for a couple of days for a short holiday with you, or the children are back home again. If you want to surprise your guests, then maybe this idea will appeal to you – round off your Easter walk with a rustic, country Easter celebration.

What to do:

Create a mossy dell on your table! A moss arrangement stands in the centre, which you can design with the help of the whole family. All of you can also bring together the other components and prepare them.

Fresh moss serves here as the background for eggs, flowers and terracotta pots. You will find moss in woods, or maybe even in your garden, or you can buy it throughout the year from your florist or garden centre. In order to protect the wooden surface of the table, you can place cling film underneath.

Dot small spring flowers – such as grape hyacinths, narcissii and daisies – and twigs which you have previously stuck into oasis (which can also be bought from your florist) across the moss. It looks pretty if the delicate flower stalks are "growing" or "tumbling" out of one or more pots.

Place the terracotta pots in the moss, and then fill them with coloured eggs or flowers.

Tip:

For preference, eggs which have been coloured with natural dyes are best for these natural table decorations. You can obtain all the colours you need from natural products such as herbs, bark and rind. Simply boil the eggs with one of the herbs or other products, and – depending on the depth of colour in the water – leave the egg in the dye until you get the shade you want. Repeat this process until you have a collection of eggs in graduated shades of colour. You can also buy natural dyes from chemists and health food shops, and they will be able to give you further advice.

Depending on the size of the table, and personal taste, other Easter decorations such as quails' eggs, little Easter bunnies or painted Easter eggs can be incorporated into the decorations.

Breakfast with fresh fruit

An invitation to breakfast on a sunny summer morning is simply wonderful. The guest is met by the aroma of fresh bread and coffee. That's the most attractive thing about breakfasting together: you have more time to spend with each other, you have the whole day before you, and breakfast can easily turn into brunch, if liked, or even an afternoon get-together over coffee. The things that you enjoy as the guest of other people can also be enjoyed when you are the hostess, as there is even pleasure to be gained from the preparations involved. A summer breakfast with lots of fresh fruit can be something special and exciting for you and your guests, and the table can be made to look very inviting with very little effort.

What to do:

If you restrict the table linen and crockery to white and shades of green, you already have the basis for a fresh effect. Of course, you can use other colours in combination with white, but the green and white combination springs to mind first because of the natural green of fruit and leaves.

The focal point of this decoration is, of course, fruit – as lush and beautiful as a bouquet of flowers. Select as many different seasonal fruits as you will need to fill a large fruit bowl. The composition should reflect your imagination and the range of fruits available at the time of year. It doesn't matter whether you use strawberries, grapes, exotic fruit or dried fruit; they are all suitable for creating this fruit bowl.

Two simple tricks create the special effects. The fruit is dusted with sieved icing sugar while it is still damp from washing. Then a few unsugared vine or strawberry leaves are pushed between the fruit for contrast. If these leaves aren't available, you can use ivy, but it must be dry and the stems must not come into contact with the fruit. Poisonous substances, which must not build up on the fruit, develop in wet ivy.

A piece of cloth (150 x 150 cm) [5 ft x 5 ft] is arranged loosely in a circle around the fruit bowl. This further emphasises the central fruit arrangement.

You can use the design theme from the centre of the table for the place settings. Place fruit and leaves on the plates and finish off with thin bands of the material used in the central decoration, draping them loosely around the plates.

Tip:

If you have invited several guests for breakfast, you can get them to help with the culinary part of the table decorations. Ask your guests to conjure up their own creations from their choice of fresh fruit and bring them with them instead of flowers.

Perhaps it is one of your most pleasant childhood memories too, of running over the golden yellow stubble fields in autumn and, with dad's help, flying a home-made kite. What a feeling of joy, happiness and excitement when your colourful kite sailed across the sky!

If you want to celebrate the next child's birthday in autumn as a kite-flying expedition, or simply want to go on an outing to the harvest fields, then this decorative idea can definitely considerably increase the quality of your time.

The red and white checked tablecloth emphasises the rustic and happy setting where your meal will be held. A few large tea towels will serve the same purpose.

Several kites – complete with reels and tails, in a range of sizes and colours - provide a background for your little buffet. It doesn't matter whether they are home-made or bought, they radiate cheerfulness and are a ready-made invitation to grab the reels and start kite flying after you have eaten together.

Smaller toy kites, in this case made of wood, serve as napkin holders. Such models can easily be made from paper or cardboard. If you like, you can use the same models as invitation cards. Stick the small kites onto a card or write on the kite itself. You will be bound to surprise your guests with an unusual invitation to an equally unusual get-together.

The hungry mouths of those present, especially if it's a child's birthday, will decide what's on the menu. Perhaps natural dishes and ingredients can emphasise the fact that it is possible to have such a good time outside in the fresh air.

What to do:

Try to find a field or meadow where the hay or straw has already been bailed but not brought in. The bales will provide ready-made tables and chairs.

Holiday atmosphere. Are you one of those people who go for long walks along the beach when on holiday, collecting shells, stones and driftwood as little treasures and mementoes of your holiday to take home? Then in principle you already have the essential ingredients for this table decoration.

What to do:

Arrange a small beach scene in the middle of your table. To avoid damage to your table, place newspaper under the sand. If you don't have a glass table top, a blue tablecloth will do just as well to represent the colour of the sea.
If you don't want to raid your child's sandpit, you can buy fine white sand cheaply from craft shops.

Scatter your holiday mementoes (mussel shells, stones, snails' shells, sea urchins, sea horses) on the sand. If you can't find any seaside knick-knacks, stones and a few mussel shells will do.

Grasses like those found amongst sand dunes will give your beach scene a particularly authentic touch. They will work to best effect if spread out under the place settings. Your florist should have several different types of grasses available.

Use white or blue glass crockery and matching napkin rings. These go particularly well with the overall decorations, because they take on the colour and transparency of water. If you haven't got any glass napkin rings, you can use a half-opened mussel. Push the napkin into the shell and fasten with a natural binding.

Autumn on the table

In late autumn, a walk through the woods or along a freshly ploughed field is always an experience for the senses. The silence all around; the soft, damp earth under your feet; the unique magnificence of the autumn colours and the misty, spicy air; the last blackberries by the side of the road. Even if some people aren't so keen on autumn, because the days draw in so quickly, such a walk is one of the special attractions of this time of year, before the cold weather arrives.

Be inspired by colourful leaves, chestnuts, acorns, roots and mushrooms. Use the stimulus which nature provides and after your walk transform them into an atmospheric autumnal table.

What to do:

Choose autumnal colours such as moss green and warm shades of yellow and brown for table linen and crockery. All the decorative elements should link into this colour scheme.

You can place moss which you have brought with you from the woods in the centre of the table as a background for the decorations. You should look for a nice piece of bark which you can place, inside uppermost, on top of the moss, and then stick a few mushrooms into the bark.

You should then scatter the various things you have found in the woods – acorns, chestnuts and nuts, together with a few small twigs with leaves around the central "nature scene". A set of antlers can also be placed on the table; although it's not exactly the done thing in hunting circles for this to happen, if you like the effect, you will surely get away with it this once.

If you want to make the decorations as a whole more "hunting, shooting and fishing" oriented, you can always use a few items from the hunting world, such as hunting horns, for decoration. Copies of pictures or old engravings with hunting scenes or similar designs are suitable for menu cards.

Tip:

If you don't have enough time to make up menu cards, simply take nice big autumn leaves, fasten small, neutral coloured cards on which you have written out the menu to them, and lay these place leaves on the place settings.

In the eighteenth and nineteenth centuries, the shepherds in Scotland would gather together in their huts, known as bothies, to tell stories, sing, drink and simply get warm.

The Scots have retained elements of this along with many other good old traditions. They still get together to talk about the day's events, to exchange news and spend some time together over a cup of tea and a snack.

Even if friends have just dropped round for no particular reason and you're only having a snack, you

may still want to decorate the table and make it look different. Then take a leaf out of the Scot's book.

What to do:

If you have a wooden table, then don't bother with a tablecloth. Wood looks good in this simple, rather rustic table decoration.

If you do use a tablecloth, then a tartan one is particularly suitable. The traditional red and green colours in tartan appear again and again in many elements of these decorations: in the crockery, candles, napkins and ribbons.

With a wooden table, the tartan appears in the ribbon tying up the napkins. Also tartan ribbons tied around bunches of holly look very attractive.

Together with red apples and perhaps a few pine cones, holly forms the "floral" decoration for this table. Above all, the table is defined by its natural charm. Artificial glitz has no place in this decoration.

Tip:

Red and green are the well-known tartan colours. But perhaps your china would match yellow or blue better? There are Scottish tartans which also contain these colours, an indication of the Viking origins of some Scottish clans, and they are just as traditionally Scottish as the more usual colours.

What on earth gets into people? They build wooden things with iron-shod runners; if it snows they head for the hills, the wooden contraption strapped to their backs; they struggle through the snow up the hill, breathe deeply when they get to the top; then their eyes light up, they leap more or less elegantly onto the sledge and thunder down into the valley at breakneck speed.

And what's it all for? Because it's loads of fun. It doesn't matter whether you are young or old, everyone has tales of sledging parties where the greatest fun was had despite the effort involved, especially when a whole gang went sledging.

But when the night descends early, cold noses and freezing feet soon drive the sledge specialists back inside, where tea, mulled wine and other treats soon help them to warm up.

If you want to surprise the home-coming sledging party with a delicious winter meal, served on a table which is almost as beautiful as the sledging slope outside but much warmer and more comfortable, then the idea for this table decoration can provide the impetus. Bring winter onto your table.

What to do:

Obviously a white, unpatterned tablecloth is best suited to providing a background for a winter scene. It isn't laid flat on the table though, because a sledging party on flat ground is no fun at all. With a few cardboard boxes or small cushions, built up under the cloth in the centre of the table, you can create a hilly landscape which provides slopes for 'sledging'.

The table is then "snow covered" from the centre out, with the help of a handful of salt. Natural salt crystals create the best glitter effect, but you can also use sugar as snow.

Decorate the hillsides with a few Christmas trees borrowed from your children's toys or bought from a specialist shop. They should also be "snow-capped", but use icing sugar this time, because it clings better to the branches.

The little sledges stand for the wintry activities, and they are filled with Christmas-time treats, to which guests can help themselves, but only after the meal!

Christmas gift tags are used as place cards; in this case they show a sledging party from olden times. The name of each guest is written on them and they are placed on top of the napkin.

Tip:

Do you want to provide your guests with a menu card, and do you feel like making an original menu card holder yourself? Make a snowman out of three balls of crumpled up paper, a little plaster of Paris and any other ingredients you can think of. Later the snowman can hold the menu card in his arms.

Children's birthdays in winter can turn out to be real celebrations of snow and sledging. If you want to decorate the table for children after the sledging party, you can use red and white paper plates. The little sledges on the table are fully laden with sweets sure to appeal to any child.

Celebrating with friends

Some friends visit frequently, some visit unexpectedly. It doesn't matter whether it's a small group of friends or a big, happy party, the laden table is always the central point.

The pictures on the following pages will show you that the table decorations can perhaps be the surprise of the evening. Cosy or cool, thoughtful or playful, cheerful or elegant, they are all based on exciting ideas.

Formerly music at home was part of domestic life. The middle classes, in the first half of the last century, met with like-minded people to enjoy music in a relaxed atmosphere.

Even if it's unfashionable now, try inviting your friends to a musical

evening at your home. It would be nice if each guest could make a musical contribution, or if everyone could sing and make music together. Of course, you can book a chamber ensemble whose music will be the highlight of the evening.

What to do:

For this table, simply use musical accoutrements, such as sheet music and instruments which are placed on the table.

Tuning forks are used as napkin holders. Alternatively you could shape bass and treble keys out of wire and then use them to decorate or hold the napkins.

For the menu cards you should copy the details onto sheet music, and place it on a music stand together with other sheets. You could also roll the menu sheet and tie it up with a ribbon, and place one on the table next to each place setting. By the way, it's not at all difficult to make sheet music look old. Just soak some cotton wool balls in

cold tea, then pat the sheet music with the cotton wool until it takes on a brownish colour. Leave to dry, then smooth flat.

You could perhaps stand the bust of a musician whom you particularly admire in the centre of the table. Use a nostalgic candelabra, which when decorated with green leaves will bring a fresh note to the table. Use large leaves and single stems of grass, pushed into oasis and arranged in a circle around the candelabra. Oasis is available from florists.

If you don't like lace-edged cloths, tulle, silver candelabra and ribbons, but prefer simple and cool design, then there is no reason why you can't express your own style on the table. "Keep cool" will challenge your creativity, whether you use scrap metal, as shown in the picture here, or other materials which suit your taste.

What to do:

An old sheet of iron is used as a table here. You may be able to borrow such sheets from a metalworker, or have a look in your cellar or garage and see if there's a sheet of metal quietly rusting away. If this is too time-consuming or "weighty" for you, a small steel or tin tray placed in the middle of the table will do just as well.

A simple chain of Christmas-tree lights laid in an abstract pattern across the table will provide little scattered points of light.

Then scatter steel or aluminium filings across the table so that they emphasise the table settings and, if possible, hide the light cables. You can get these filings from a metal workshop. You might even get them for free.

Take care, because steel filings have sharp edges. Use them carefully as decorations, and don't put them in the dustbin afterwards.

You can also twist small filings into napkin rings, which will surely strike your guests as unusual. Alternatively you can use galvanised copper wire or thick soldering wire, which can be wrapped imaginatively around the rolled napkin.

If you want to extend the use of steel to your other decorations, you can quickly make a flower vase and tray without taking a great deal of time or trouble. You need two cheap sheets of stainless steel from a builder's merchant (sheet thickness 0.5 mm, 33 x 33 cm square), which you can bend into any shape you like using your hands. To make the tray all four sides are bent upwards asymmetrically. To make the flower vase, two corners are bent towards and to one side of each other, to make an open tube shape.

Tip:

Serve a cold drink, which matches the table decorations, as an aperitif – such as iced vodka or schnapps. You can achieve a special effect by rinsing glasses in cold water and then putting them in the freezer. The iced glasses look particularly good when filled with brightly coloured cocktails, such as blue Curaçao or Campari.

Bella Italia

Either you've just come back from a holiday in Italy or you've got it still to look forward to. Or maybe you simply love the Italian way of life, relaxed and friendly, cheerful and colourful. Of course, you're just as keen on Italian cuisine as well, which is so much more than just pizza and pasta. What about the typical antipasti, and many delicious Mediterranean specialities, or "formaggio" (cheese) to round off a meal, and wonderful red wine to drink?

Get together with your friends for a "Bella Italia" evening, and give your table an appropriate southern flavour. You simply must have tomatoes, red wine and, of course, spaghetti!

What to do:

Use the colours of Italy by laying three lengths of fabric over the table in such a way that they look like the Italian flag. You should use these three colours for the napkins as well, preferably as a contrast to the background (e.g., green on white and red on green).

You then arrange tomatoes, basil and different types of pasta decoratively on the table. What is important is that you should be generous with the decorations. Don't hesitate to take a handful of tomatoes and penne pasta and scatter both over the table. Spaghetti and macaroni can easily be set up as a game of "pick-up-sticks", tied with a ribbon in the Italian national colours.

Your invitations to guests can hint at what they should expect; try little home-made packets of uncooked pasta, tied with ribbons in the Italian national colours with an invitation card attached. They are easy to make, original and tempt the appetite.

Tip:

You could also place a small Italian travel or food guide on guests' place settings, as a little gift for them to take home. Furthermore, you could use the food guide as the menu card for the evening.

Do you prefer French food? Well, surely your imagination will come up with ideas for a French-style table, and you must certainly be familiar with the colours of the Tricolor.

Candlelight dinner

The story goes, according to the ancient Greeks, that roses should not be considered in the same way as other flowers and plants, because they came into the world together with the goddess of love, Aphrodite. Thus both Aphrodite and roses became symbols of love among mankind.

They come together again here on this table: roses and a small marble bust of Aphrodite. In your personal situation you can use something which reminds you both of an event that has happened to you, or some other little thing which will ensure that not only is the table beautifully set, but that it also shows something personal.

What to do:

Make your table atmospheric, but don't overload it with decorations. The central point can be provided by a candelabra whose candles shed just enough light. Fine china, stylish glasses and other items in silver, combined with candlelight, will give the table a very elegant appearance.

The china used in this table setting, with its complex, filigree pattern (a stylised representation of the Gardens of Versailles) lends additional romanticism to the overall impression. However, if your own china is less

complex, or even plain white, it will look much more special if you set silver-plated place plates under it. If you don't already have some, such place plates are well worth investing in; they are no longer reserved for hotels and restaurants.

You could choose either roses which match the colour of the table linen and crockery, or ones which are in conscious contrast to it. Cut the stems off close to the base of the flowers and arrange them on the table.

You can increase the demonstration of affection described above with other little loving gestures, or decoratively wrapped gifts. Unwrapping such gifts provides a little something extra for the evening.

Tip:

When preparing the food, be careful to avoid the necessity of having to get up frequently during the meal to work in the kitchen. What is the point of the most beautiful *dîner à deux* if your guest is left sitting on his own for ages, not knowing whether he should come to the kitchen to help you and keep you company, or whether he should stay at the table?

Holiday – Buen Viaje!

Whether you are hot on the trail of Don Quixote or Velasquez, or simply spending relaxing days in the warm Spanish sun, it can still be exciting to act as a hostess on a small scale when you're staying in foreign lands.

Native specialities, exotic flowers and leaves can be combined by simple means to produce unusual arrangements. The lifestyle and culinary specialities which you see on holiday can be reflected in your decorations.

What to do:

The table impresses with its simplicity, it radiates atmosphere without too many frills, and the charm of the Mediterranean is typified by the rich colours of the flowers, framed in elegant white. As a final touch the napkins are held together with a strip of palm leaf.

The table takes its colour from bougainvillea, which is found everywhere along the side of the road. Here it is laid out on banana leaves, which do an excellent job as place mats in the centre of the table. Banana leaves are not as common as bougainvillea, but there are many other large leaves available which are equally useful and decorative as a background.

Tapas is the typical Spanish delicacy which is served as a starter or as a snack with wine. Traditionally it is served on a small saucer which goes under the wine glass, but more often nowadays it is served in small bowls on the table so that you can help yourself. Depending on the choice and how hungry you are, you can fill yourself up with these delicacies. The tapas dishes used here are placed in the centre of the table.

If you don't want to load the table with tapas dishes at the start of the evening, you can start with two or three specialities and serve different dishes during the course of the evening.

House-moving brunch

You must surely be familiar with the scenario – you've moved to a new house and would like to do something to thank the stalwart friends who were there when you needed them. Or your friends are all so desperate to inspect your new home that you're left with no choice but to hold your house-warming party in the middle of packing cases and rolls of carpet.

The last thing you have on your mind is inviting people to brunch amongst the confusion of boxes and shelves, pictures and suitcases. The fact that everything is all over the place, that you're constantly hunting for mislaid items, that there are stacks of boxes – usually in your way – none of this would make you think of stopping in the middle of it all and restoring body and soul with a glass of champagne and your feet up for ten minutes.

But it can work! With a bit of courage and a dash of spontaneity, which you should expect of your guests as well, a house-moving brunch of this kind can easily fall into the category of a gastronomic experience. The great thing is that people won't expect the setting to be perfect. The free and easy combination of all that is best in breakfast and lunch, combined with the unusual setting, is bound to appeal to your guests.

What to do:

The packing cases, which are bound to be plentiful, are used here as tables, stools, buffet tables, a plant stand and anything else you can think of.

Because your table linen is probably packed away somewhere, you can always use clean dust sheets as tablecloths. This saves you the trouble of having to hunt out your tablecloths, and the bother of washing them afterwards.

Toy furniture from a doll's house, which you can buy in toy shops, is wrapped in tissue paper and can be used as a decoration for this house-moving brunch. The invitations can also be made with little effort. Invitation cards and envelopes are cut or folded out of cardboard and tissue

paper so that they look like miniature packing cases. You can then photocopy the invitation or write it by hand.

Tip:

The buffet table shouldn't just be one long surface like a pasting table. There should be different levels; some things should stand on the floor, others higher up on a pile of boxes, and some at an intermediate level. Don't be afraid to build a scene around your buffet, it will look more exciting and will be better suited to the informal occasion.

The finale of the opera takes your breath away, the orchestra puts everything into it and all the actors are gathered on the stage. The curtain falls, and there is prolonged applause; the evening at the opera was once again a wonderful experience – but, as so often happens, it was all over far too quickly.

You can change that by planning a finale using an operatic theme for your table design. Invite your friends to join you for a post-opera dinner to bring the evening to a close. The table is your backcloth, using items from the world of opera for your theme. You're the director here, this is your stage setting. Curtain up for a table at the opera!

What to do:

An old bright red velvet cloth thrown loosely over the table is your tablecloth. Fine china on silver place plates, engraved glasses and orchids as the floral decoration emphasise the table's character.

The connection between the table setting and the opera is created by placing objects from the world of theatre on the table – small props, crowns, masks, gloves, as well as opera glasses and the programme from the evening. You may have some of these things at home already, but you can borrow them for a modest sum from theatrical suppliers.

Old-fashioned face masks can be used as place cards for your guests. You can write the names of your guests on them with a silver pen. These place cards are particularly effective and your guests are sure to add to the evening's merriment by trying on their masks. Let the actor in you take over, with the table as your stage for the evening.

Tip:

If you have a recording of the music from the opera, why not play this for your guests during the meal as a pleasant reminder of your evening together?

Do you enjoy board and card games? Are you and expert at draughts, or do you prefer whist and mah jong? Perhaps you are a wizard at chess, or like to meet up with friends for bridge parties?

If so, then you could turn your home into a private gaming room and surprise your guests with a table decoration which continues the gaming theme throughout the meal to the games afterwards.

What to do:

Use the familiar game boards from your collection. If you are using different types of boards you should ensure that the overall decorative effect of these and the other decorations does not clash. In this case it's a good idea to use just a few pieces from the games as decorations. Scatter pieces, dice and playing cards across the table. You can also construct very attractive card houses on the table which will no doubt tempt your guests to have a go at building them.

You can easily make a napkin ring which tones with with the colour scheme out of two strips of stiff paper. The strips should be about 60 cm [2 feet] long and 2cm [1 inch] wide. Lay one strip on top of the other and then fold them together to make a concertina, as illustrated. If you glue all four ends together you will get a ring which can then be slipped over the napkins.

Red roses or carnations are always associated with elegant casinos in films. Simply place a few flowers on the decorated table.

Tip:

If you can't find enough game boards, you can achieve an equally decorative effect by placing dominoes in a pattern around the place setting.

The magic of roses

If you are a bit on the romantic side and love to have roses on your table, leave your vase in the cupboard for once and arrange the colourful blooms in a different way. A sea of flowers like this is attractive to behold, smells heavenly and furthermore can be fun to put together.

What to do:

Here a large glass bowl is filled with water. Roses, single rose petals and floating candles in between decorate the surface of the water. A few petals scattered randomly across the table emphasise the impression created by the flower bowl and mean it doesn't look quite so alone in the middle of the table.

Even if roses are best suited to this arrangement, you can of course use other flowers. You should look at the setting for the flower bowl to decide whether to use strong colours or pastel shades.

Tip:

You can strengthen the flowery, perfumed nature of this rose table decoration if you add a couple of drops of rose oil to the flowers, which will really add to the effect of the scent. Your guests will not fail to be impressed by this pretty combination.

Just a few years ago decorative lengths of fabric of the width and quality shown here were thought to cost too much for any but the most expensive, professionally decorated tables.

All that has changed. Today you should be able to get table runners in many sizes, fabric qualities, patterns and shadings, in shops which offer decorative products at reasonable prices. As an alternative you can easily make your own.

What to do:

When buying or making your table runners, make sure they match the colours and shapes of the tablecloth, crockery and other accoutrements. If everything tones in nicely or an attractive colour contrast is achieved, then you are more than halfway to a successful table decoration.

Place the runner lengthways down the centre of the table. Separate bows made of the same material are added at each end, and are fastened to the runner and the tablecloth using safety pins or dressmaker's pins.

Big blooms centred in green leaves and grasses add spots of colour to brighten up the setting. The flowers used here are peonies, but you can also use hydrangeas, roses, gerbera or other flowers.

Tip:

Plan the arrangements so that you have time just before your guests arrive to take the flowers out of water and place them on the table or fasten them onto the bows. Even better, buy the little phials which you can get from your florist to hold single blooms. In this way you'll be able to spend time with your guests and the table decorations will stay fresh while you serve drinks.

"Oh, how charming!" your guests might say when they see this table, as they are reminded of quiet, relaxing moments watching a family of ducks on a still pond. This table setting will help you to revive that feeling of peace and relaxation for your guests.

What to do:

You don't need to take the mirror from your dressing table to put this decorative idea into practice as you can buy mirrors in all shapes and sizes from DIY stores and handicraft shops.

Ducks are now collectables, so if you haven't got any you should be able to find wooden ones easily in shops which sell accessories, as well as flowers or furnishings, and these will be ideally suited to this idyllic little pond scene.

Frame the mirror with a few green leaves and grasses which look like the plants around the edges of a pond.

Tip:

A few night lights placed on the mirror create an especially pretty effect of reflected light.

Stone on stone

Have you ever seen the marvellous stony shores of the Scandinavian fjords, or the wonderful marble shapes along the Aegean coast? Have you ever wandered along a beach, your eyes glued to the ground, picking up attractive stones until your jacket pockets bulge? Then you too are affected by the magic of these stones shaped by the waves. Such stones make you want to look at them, pick them up and stroke their smooth surfaces. Your collection of stones can be used as a simple but unusual table decoration.

What to do:
Group together two or three dozen stones which you have collected (or even bought) in the centre of the table to create a rockery. The stark impression is relieved by hibiscus flowers, which can be put in little water phials (available from florists) or placed between the stones just before your guests arrive. You can of course use other flowers – such as gerbera, hydrangeas, lilies or marguerites.

Tip:
If you want to use candles, use night lights to create an interesting play of light and shadow between the stones and flowers.

A touch of tulle

In most cases the classic bouquet of flowers is still the centrepiece in any table decoration, yet if you have any sense of style at all you will realise that it is not enough just to put a vase of cut flowers on the table. Pretty, tasteful bouquets are small, easily achievable works of art which can make a considerable impression on the overall table design and leave a pleasant impression on your guests.

What to do:

Consciously select a bunch of flowers from your florist which teams up with the shapes and colours in your china, so that they go well together but contrast strongly with the underlying tablecloth. If, for example, you are using a dark background then the pale pastel colours of the flowers will be displayed to greater effect.

The effect is enhanced by the use of matching tulle, which is draped around the vase so that the whole arrangement comes together.

Tulle bows tied around the napkins provide additional splashes of colour on the table to round off the overall design.

Basket weaving

Elephant grass and green bamboo are amongst the materials which are rarely used as table decorations in the home, which is a shame because they are very suitable for quick and effective table settings and because their uncluttered lines make an unusual and striking centrepiece. Elephant grass and bamboo can be bought from most florists.

What to do:

Using elephant grass or thin bamboo, weave a simple shape in a basket pattern, fastening the canes at various points with thin wire, and place in the centre of the table. Tie up a few bundles of reeds and place these underneath the basket weaving to give the whole thing more height. The weaving is slightly raised up off the table and, depending on the lighting, will cast interesting shadows on the tablecloth underneath. Finally, place little bunches of wild flowers and grasses on top of the weaving. In the picture I have used cornflowers and lady's mantle. Depending on the occasion and the choice of flowers available in your florist's shop, you could turn this into an exotic decoration by using figs, for example, and other exotic fruit, and by arranging appropriate flowers on top of the weaving.

Tip:

If your basket weaving is very firm and securely tied with wire, you could even use it as a tray for small bowls and dishes.

The finest Savoy cabbage

Decorating with vegetables instead of flowers – many people turn up their noses at this suggestion. But have you ever thought that a combination of Savoy cabbage, grapes, horse chestnuts and apples could create a quick and cheap alternative to a bunch of flowers on the table? Furthermore, your guests are hardly likely to overlook this decoration, because Savoy cabbage doesn't appear on the table like this every day, does it?

What to do:

All the ingredients for this decoration only cost a couple of pounds and some of them can be consumed after use. Apples, grapes and cabbage come from the greengrocer or market; horse chestnuts and ivy from the woods; bear grass from the florist. The only other things you need are a simple wire basket and a little thin wire.

In the picture the Savoy cabbage, grapes, horse chestnuts and apples are simply arranged around a wire basket. Bear grass is shaped into little nests and fastened with the thin (green) wire. The apples are placed in the nests as a splash of colour against the green cabbage. The rest of the decorations depend on your imagination. Let your creative instincts run riot.

Tip:
An apple will look especially shiny if you rub a little fat onto it and then polish it with a cloth.

Water lilies

Water lilies speak for themselves – their unmistakeable appearance and power to attract make them a perfect decoration for your table. Let these magical blooms dominate the centre of your table, concentrate your table decorations around them and avoid the temptation to add anything else.

What to do:
Place the water lilies in a large, glass bowl lined with white pebbles. Scatter a few pebbles around the bowl. They will look particularly attractive if you spray them with gold paint.

Take up the theme of the arrangement in the centre of the table with the place settings. Place the napkins on top of big green leaves and tie the two together with gold cord.

Tip:
Keep the table simple. The food and drink can be passed round and then put to one side on a little table. In this way your table will seem uncluttered during the meal and your guests will feel the benefit.

You can have a table setting without flowers. Instead of using a faded cyclamen or an azalea from the window sill to decorate the table, why don't you find other items for the display? Candles, for example.

Often a candle is stuck on the table setting at the last minute so that it looks a bit more cheerful, but in this case candles are the most important thing on the table. They form the central point and everything else is grouped around them.

What to do:

You will almost certainly have different types of candlesticks in your house. Dare to combine these candlesticks to make a table decoration which strikes your guests as a planned harmonious arrangement. Use candlesticks made from the same material – either silver, china, brass or wood, or glass as we have used here.

Sharp contrasts are equally effective; you could combine candlesticks made from different types of materials. In fact you can do whatever you like.

Marbles, which can be bought cheaply in all sizes and colours, complement the candle arrangement. Of course, you can use little balls made of other materials (china, wood or brass) to scatter in between the candlesticks.

Tip:

The group of candles is most effective if it is allowed to stand on its own in the centre of the table without jostling for space with dishes and bottles. Keep plenty of room between the other items on the table and your lighting group.

Ribbon star

Guests who phone you up to tell you they're on their way to visit you can cause hustle and bustle and even panic in your household, as well as delight at the unexpected visit. The table has to be set, the house given a semblance of tidiness and a cake or some pastries have to appear on the double.

If you don't want just to set the table in such a situation, but would rather put a little more effort into it, it's a good idea to use decorations which are within easy reach, but which still demonstrate your personal style.

This table uses things which you will find in your cupboards or which you can quickly grab from the garden or the nearest bush.

What to do:
Here decorative strips of fabric or ribbons for gift wrapping in different shades of colour and widths are simply laid across the table to form a star pattern. You will have to decide which colours go with your crockery and which suit the time of year.

To hold everything in place use a shallow bowl in the centre of the table placed underneath the ribbons. The ribbons run through the centre of the bowl and are held in place by a few stones. Then fill the bowl with water and place flowers of any kind, in this case sunflowers, in between the stones. With very little effort you will have created an eye-catching centrepiece for your table.

If you have to put something together quickly there's often a problem with regard to which vase goes best with the crockery and tablecloth. Often there isn't one which is suitable. But before you settle for second best, there is another alternative. You don't have to use a vase to decorate your table; other containers – such as bowls, jugs or bottles, for example – are often much better suited to a setting which is a little out of the ordinary.

What to do:

A row of empty green bottles makes an effective table decoration. Old wine or champagne bottles covered in a layer of dust are particularly stylish, especially if they have old-fashioned labels. You can buy them from junk shops for a few pounds.

You can be restrained with the flowers here. Just a single flower head, or a few placed at different heights in the bottles, will have such an effect that the whole arrangement will come across as a stylish, carefully thought-out still life.

Tip:

Easily made labels that describe the dishes to be served, or the wine which will accompany them, can give old bottles without labels a special role. If you stick the menu labels on the bottles, this unusual table decoration will have your guests eagerly anticipating the coming meal.

Al-fresco dining

When the days get longer and warmer we are drawn outside as if by a magnet. Then some people feel the desire to enjoy, for once, something a bit more special outside than an ice-cream or a squashed sandwich.

The examples on the next few pages will show you how to create interesting table decorations outdoors using simple methods and with limited effort. You will experience how stylishly such tables can be set.

The British were passionate about their picnics in the last century. Most weekends they went off into the countryside in pairs or in groups, but the whole experience could be summed up by "grass in the salad, sand in the butter, wasps in the fruit juice and endless flies"!

Despite these various misfortunes the picnic has remained one of the favourite ways to get together down through the years.

Not every picnic is a picnic, by the way. A couple of sandwiches by the side of the road have very little to do with the original concept. Nearly one hundred and forty years ago picnics were governed by rules of etiquette, for example regarding the kind of people who should join the party. *Chamber's Journal* of 6 June 1857 clearly states: "A picnic group should consist primarily of young men and women, two or three older male persons are permissible if they are very good-natured; a couple of pleasant children and one, but only one, nice old lady whom the company should entrust in advance with supervising organisation of the picnic, if possible, and to whom dictatorial powers have been granted in this regard ...".

Well, the town park isn't Ascot, and today a picnic can be as different as those who are organising it wish to make it. But perhaps you will discover the charm of an outing in the style of olden days. Gather together whatever you can find in the way of old-fashioned accoutrements and invite your friends to a country gathering, turn-of-the-century style.

What to do:
You're talking table decorations without a table here, so all your guests can get involved. Ask them to bring part of the provender in the form of old glasses, baskets and terrines.

You can put together the crockery, glassware and cutlery and stow it away in a suitable wicker basket. You don't need a fully fitted picnic basket for this, or a porcelain dinner service. Decorative, rustic china, which combines easily with other utensils, will be just as useful.
If you wrap each cutlery place setting in a napkin, it will be ready for each guest. You can do this at home and it means you have one less thing to worry about at the beginning of the picnic.

Look round your house, and ask friends for accessories from Grandma's era: straw boaters, walking sticks, and song books. The nice thing is that these items are not just decorative, they can also be used.

Tip:

Your imagination will help you decide what you should offer to eat and drink; or an old-fashioned cookery book or even Grandma may help, if she still remembers the recipes for picnic delicacies.

Don't be afraid to ask around so you

can come up with a tasty alternative to sandwiches and quiche.

Do you like visiting the countryside, tracking down plants and animals and perhaps spending a few happy, relaxed hours in the open-air?

If you enjoy rustic meals in the country, then this table decoration will surely fire your imagination as a hostess. Enchant your guests with the magic of a rural still life on the table. This decorative idea can be put into practice very easily in any little green corner.

What to do:

The materials and objects used here should all reflect the natural, rural atmosphere.

Rustic crockery is best suited to such a hearty country meal. You can also use plain, undecorated china which does not contrast with the other decorations.

You may already have found a suitable source of old agricultural accessories (in miniature is best), or you will give yourself time to browse in second-hand shops or toy shops. It can be very satisfying to add to your collection of hay wagons, tools, milk churns and various animals over the course of time, so that one day you will be able to produce them on the table for such an occasion.

Add to your decorations with fruit according to season. In this case the food should not be brought to the table but should be part of the decorations, tempting people to pick and choose whatever they like. For example, you could use home-made bread, apples and cherries as shown on this table.

If you like, you could add butter, eggs and vegetables, as well as small pots with little bunches of herbs (parsley, dill and chives). This extends the menu and adds a touch of freshness to the arrangement.

The rural still life is rounded off with a bundle of corn placed underneath the hay wagon and a pot full of daisies or other wild flowers.

You can take a few ears of corn from the bundle and use them to tie up the napkins which have been folded into a triangle.

Monet's famous water lily pictures convey some of the magic of the garden which the great painter owned: the bold, wild growth of grasses and bushes on the banks, the reeds blowing gently in the breeze and the play of light on water.

You can still find such idyllic spots today. You might have to look a bit harder for them but they are there and when you do find them they are even more enchanting, making you want to stay and lose yourself in their picturesque beauty.

If you want to arrange something special, then choose such an idyllic setting for a dinner for two or four, pack up everything you will need and invite your guests to dine with you on the shores of the lake.

What to do:

An old lace tablecloth, well suited to this scene, will add a romantic touch. It is laid over a tablecloth in a solid colour, which matches the colour of the crockery.

The combination of colours in the surroundings, green and blue, is picked up in the table. A steel-blue dinner service is used, and blue coloured glasses. They combine with the green of the fruit and grasses which are placed on the table.

If you have an étagère, this can be used as a fruit bowl, giving the whole table setting a little height. The centre of the étagère is surrounded by leaves picked from the shores of the lake.

You should also use plants from the shore for the remaining floral decorations. In this case a few long stems of pampas grass are laid across the table. On the one hand this looks pretty, and on the other you have the advantage that you don't have to bring along a vase.

Many shore-line scenes would be incomplete without fishermen, who are already out on the banks early in the morning, whatever the weather, staring into the still water. If the sight of them inspires you, you can easily express this in the table decorations. Tie little fish hooks or wooden fish to the napkins.

Tip:

Of course, for this al-fresco dinner you must make sure that you can carry everything you need and stow it away in your car. For this reason you need folding garden furniture, and the meal can be restricted to a few delicious morsels which can be prepared well in advance, are easily packed away and can be arranged attractively on site. The only thing you shouldn't stint on is the decorative materials. It will definitely be worth transporting them.

Monet can give you a hand with the invitation cards as well. You can buy his water lily paintings as postcards. Use these cards as your invitations and give your guests a taste of what is to come.

For art lovers who don't go to every opening day but who still like to visit galleries and museums, it doesn't take much effort to arrange something special – a spontaneous museum visit.

After visiting the exhibition you can meet friends and like-minded people in the open air near the museum to talk about what you've seen. Over a glass of wine you exchange impressions and express your artistic points of view, whether original or not, before you have to part company.

The table decorations which suit such an occasion are especially effective if they clearly reflect the tone of the exhibition. Contemporary or avant-garde, factual or dramatised, colourful or pastel shades, cool or even with Baroque elements in homage to old masters. Let yourself be inspired by the exhibition pieces.

What to do:

Drawing paper from a roll, available from specialist shops, is used both for a tablecloth and a canvas here. This tablecloth should not just lie there, but should truly reflect the tone of the museum visit and should be painted or written on; in other words, it should be a work of art.

As a motif, place brushes, pencils, wax crayons, tempera paints and other painting equipment on the table.

An additional stimulus can be provided by little objets d'art or exhibition posters which are also placed on the table.

If the decorations and other design elements appear too stark against the tablecloth, a colourful bunch of wild flowers with cornflowers and carnations will swiftly add the necessary freshness to liven up the table.

Tip:

If you want to hold your post-museum meeting in the museum grounds, then you should enquire whether this is possible and obtain permission. In this way you will avoid unpleasant surprises during the convivial get-together.

Almost every exhibition is announced by posters, which you can collect privately. Or you can buy picture postcards of the exhibits at the exhibition. Both are useful sources of material from which you can make invitations to your meeting. If you don't use them as an invitation, then the posters will be put to equally good use as a memento of your museum visit or as an eye-catching display on an easel.

Traditional celebrations

Life's celebrations are made up of weddings, christenings, and birthdays galore.

Here you will find inspiration for the next occasion, ideas for special table decorations, tips to avoid the repetitiveness that some traditional celebrations can tend towards, as well as helpful advice on the little details.

A Wedding –
one of life's
high points

A wedding celebration is truly something special. Nothing is left to chance. For you as the bride and groom, and for your guests it should be beautiful and exciting, a truly unforgettable celebration, and – together with the wedding ceremony – the wedding breakfast is the most important part of a weddding celebration.

The menu or buffet is planned in detail with the restaurant or catering service. There should be something special for old and young, it should be light, so people feel like dancing afterwards, and the wine list should tempt even the connoisseurs.

However, the table setting is far too often the "poor relation" when it comes to the preparations. If you leave the table setting to the caterers, you will get a nicely set table, but one which is also, unfortunately, rather impersonal. In order to avoid this, include the table settings in your plans and design an overall theme, which covers the floral decorations in church, the table settings and the invitations and place cards, so they all bear the same "personal seal". This is your day. Your imagination, coupled with the professional's expertise, should make it the celebration of your dreams.

Take inspiration from old customs and traditions, the time of year or the location of your wedding celebrations. A wedding ceremony in an old village church is an open invitation to a concluding celebration in the rustic setting of a barn; a church by a lake suggests a boat ride for everyone; and a castle chapel leads to thoughts of a castle ball.

For example, the table in these pictures shows a setting based on a reception in an old country house. The ambience was of course heavily influenced by the decor and colours. The table decorations echo the colours and style of the room, but nevertheless express an individual nature through small details.

If you match your decorative ideas to the style of the room in advance, you will make a pleasant overall impression on your guests with them.

What to do:

The classic bridal colour, white, provides an elegant background for the table linen, porcelain and napkins. Silver place plates, framed by silver cutlery and with silver candelabra in the centre of the table, emphasise the celebratory atmosphere. Ribbons and bows in white lace lend a delicate charm to the table, which creates a link to the reason for the celebration, the marriage of the happy couple. The luxuriant garland of fruits, flowers and leaves which is laid along the table is the 'pièce de résistance'. It catches the eye, whether the design is rustic or elegant, whether the colours are bright or restrained, with exotic blossoms or wild flowers. The garland on this table contains grapes, chrysanthemums, roses, veronica, asters, Doris Reika, sedum and hops. You need experience to produce such a garland, so don't try to cut corners. Leave it to the professionals, but do give clear instructions regarding your requirements.

Organising the seating plan for your wedding can be very stressful, but a successful seating plan can be decisive in ensuring that your guests enjoy themselves and leave with pleasant memories of the event. You really should make the effort, and draw up place cards for your plan. If you like, your place cards can contain a personal message for your guests, reflecting events from the childhood and adolescence of the bridal couple, for example.

Tip:

The table setting design is innovative, but three or four glasses at each place setting can often lead to a cluttered look. In order to avoid clutter, set only one glass per place setting to start with, and change it as necessary, depending on what your guests are drinking.

You can have shorter garlands made up to decorate the backs of the bride's and groom's chairs, or to festoon over a door and to lay on a window sill.

The high point of a christening is the actual ceremony, not the meal afterwards. It is nice if the overall decorative theme reflects the occasion, and the little guest of honour.

The christening party is almost as traditional as the ceremony itself. The celebration often takes place in someone's home, because it is more personal and often easier to organise in this way if there are small children present.

A christening is the first major celebration in many people's lives and so the overall design, and particularly that of the table, should always place the spotlight on the most important person. Give your imagination free reign and let your thoughts stray to things which make the hearts of children beat a little faster. Ships and sailors, beach toys, toy cars, doll's houses with "proper" furniture, daisy chains, furry toy animals; all these can be used as themes for a table decoration.

What to do: a table for the son and heir

"Hello sailor!" A blue and white themed table decoration with simple styling and lots of home-made items can act as a personalised greeting to the christening candidate.

A blue and white striped cloth in the centre of the table represents the water on which several boats are sailing. You can make these yourself in various sizes by folding them out of paper as you did when you were a child. If you have problems remembering how to do it, many handicraft books have illustrations which will show you how. The fleet will sail more safely on the table if each boat is pinned to the tablecloth.

Little wooden toy boats which you have brought back from holiday, or which you can buy cheaply in toy shops, are also very decorative.

The menu cards at each place setting are designed to look like a sailor's outfit, and with a little skill you can make them yourself out of card and satin ribbon. They will provide a pleasant memento for your guests to take home.

A family christening

being christened, which you can make yourself with a little time and effort. The best template for a silhouette is a photograph taken in profile. The head should be carefully cut out of the photograph and is used as a template on black paper. All you need is a bit of patience and a steady hand.

Tip:

One lovely tradition is planting a tree for the child on the day of the christening. The first "fruits" on the tree are little cards which are hung on the tree, containing good luck messages from the guests. The cards can be put ready on the dining table so the guests have plenty of time to think up a suitable inscription. If liked, the table decorations can be based on this theme.

What to do: the table for the little lady

Distinctive and stylish, colours and shapes with lovely, delicate charm – a personal greeting to the young lady.

Delicate shades of pale pink are reserved for the tablecloth and napkins; the crockery is white; ivy, roses and ribbons are in the same colour as the table linen – these are the design elements in this decoration.

The focal point of this table is provided by a large silver dish which is filled with rose heads. Don't worry if the bowl is a little taller than the other items, this will draw everything together.

Small wreaths of flowers, about 10 cm [4 inches] in diameter, which you can either make yourself or have made up by a florist, are positioned at equal distances along the table. You should ensure that the colour tones with the background colour of the table.

The individual elements are brought together by strands of ivy, so that the decorations combine together in a natural whole. Use small strands of ivy as napkin rings. Before using the ivy you should wash and dry it thoroughly.

The decorations are personalised with the menu card in each place setting. The card is decorated with a silhouette of the child who is

A different kind of Christmas – American style

Glimmer, glitter, glamour and gaudy colours – is this an American Christmas? You might think so if you were to visit a shopping mall in the run-up to Christmas, but Christmas is not as commercialised everywhere in America as that which you see in the shopping malls would lead you to believe. Americans do tend to go to town more on decorations, but it doesn't have to be kitsch or tasteless.

If you'd like to try a different style of table decoration this Christmas, then why not American-style?

What to do:

You will certainly have a couple, if not all of the ingredients for this table design already. You need Santa Claus, and a string of coloured lights, edible decorations, lots of brightly coloured baubles and gold tinsel.

The whole spectacular should be founded on a plain tablecloth. On this table the cloth has a metallic shimmer as a "gleaming" background for the gaudy table. Golden stars and confetti sprinkled on the table emphasise this impression and, with the right lighting, create a wonderful glitter effect.

The chain of lights is placed in the middle of the table, surrounded by a golden garland which hides the wire and shimmers with golden glints from the lights. You should arrange the cable so that it passes under the table by your seat, and so that it doesn't get in the way of your guests.

If you like, you can also arrange brightly coloured baubles in the garland. Don't be afraid to mix lots of different colours, but the baubles should all be made of the same material. When positioning them take care that the colour

of each bauble harmonises with the Christmas-tree light next to it.

In America, Christmas wouldn't be Christmas without Santa Claus. He appears on a golden sleigh, loaded with sweets or with little packages for your guests to unwrap.

The napkins should match the colour of the tablecloth. They are shaped into a cornet and held in position with a golden cord. You can also hide a little surprise gift for your guests in the napkins. You can get the cord in haberdashery or soft furnishing shops.

Tip:

Make it into a real occasion by dressing for dinner, even if you don't usually do so, but do indicate this to your guests on the invitations. The heady atmosphere and finery of your guests' attire will be sure to make it a special evening.

A birthday celebration fresh from the drawing board

Table decorations can tell a story - either to suit the occasion, or with reference to the guests, the host or the hostess. The example here is for the birthday of an architect, which is celebrated in a fitting setting.

The table here is not meant to be a work desk, but one for relaxation. The materials and equipment which surround the birthday boy or girl at work appear here and act as interesting conversation pieces.

What to do:

Of course, the basis of the table should be plans or blueprints spread across the table. Don't be afraid to lay plans and drawings at angles across each other. Your guests will have more to discover and the individual plans won't look like place mats. You can also position a few rolled-up blueprints decoratively on the table.

If you have a model building, this will be great as an exhibit. It shouldn't be too big though, otherwise it will attract too much attention and detract from your guests, which certainly won't be what you intended.

Other drawing equipment such as pencils, compasses, scissors, set square and ruler and whatever else you can think of complement the decorations. It is important not to overload the table with decorations. It shouldn't look like a table which needs a good tidy, but as though it has been designed purposefully.

The napkins can be rolled into pipes and piled together to form a pyramid, so guests can take one at will. A sprig of a plant typically planted around new buildings can be pushed into the pile of napkins.

The place cards are made of cards with cut-outs in the shape of buildings in classic architectural styles or similar designs. You can buy different kinds from good stationers. The guests' names are either written on the cards in silver pen, or printed on using a stencil.

Tip:

The birthday celebrant's profession or hobby can inspire lots of other variations in the table decorations. Toy money and stocks and shares, computer lists and calculators can be used for someone who works in a bank; gardening fans will find old engravings of flowers and plants, while pots of herbs and a toy watering can serve as a vase on the table. Just use your imagination.

Memories – the good old days

It doesn't matter whether you've led an eventful life or a quiet one – attaining 50 or 60 years of age is a perfect opportunity to remember countless little events. This is most enjoyable at home with your family or good friends of long standing who have been with you through the years.

It can be very interesting if you extract anecdotes and stories which you have never heard before from the older members of your family, using old photographs, letters or other souvenirs. Make the most of the next birthday or celebration to have a chat about the good old days, and use the decorations specifically to create a topic of conversation.

What to do:

Use old family china as decoration for the table. If an old service has been ravaged by the depredations of time, as so often happens, then don't worry about combining it with items from a more modern service which matches it.

If you use coloured table linen rather than a white cloth, you will avoid the rather formal and strict appearance, giving the table more life and lending it greater expression. Here, a deep lilac moiré cloth is thrown loosely across the table and complemented by matching tulle in the centre. If you put the family china on such a "rumpled" cloth, you will soon have the first topic of conversation, "We didn't do that in my day!"

Old family mementoes and little gifts are then scattered under or on top of the tulle. How much of a voyage of discovery this will prove to be for your guests depends on your imagination and how successful you are in hunting through old drawers and cupboards.

Use old photographs as place cards. The guests will find their places when they recognise themselves in the photo, or see something which recalls a particular memory, which they can then talk about.

Tip:

How about giving the birthday boy or girl a bouquet of memories? When you invite the guests, ask them to bring a single flower of their choice (a single rose, a carnation, etc.). There should be a card tied to the flower with a message regarding a specific event or memory which relates to the special occasion. All the flowers, with the attached cards, are then put together in a bouquet on the table, no doubt evoking a host of different memories.

Finishing touches

Planning – think first, then act

You start with a good idea.

If you only have a vague idea, turn to paper and pencil. A firm design concept can often develop from just a passing thought. There are three steps to achieving this. As a first stage, make a note of everything which you could do. The second stage is to mark what you would like to do on this occasion, and then outline how you intend to carry it out.

Write everything down, even the little trifling things which often get forgotten during preparations and then don't get done at all. It is always worth writing out such tiny details.

If you are doing a complex table decoration it is worth writing out a timetable, counting down to the big day, with greeting your guests as the final item.

Materials – obtain them in advance

Check in your cupboards to see if you have enough crockery, especially if you are serving several courses; whether you have enough glasses and if they are sparkling clean; whether you have enough cutlery and servers, and whether the silver needs cleaning; whether the tablecloth needs ironing, or if you have the correct number of napkins and whether they are freshly laundered and starched; whether you have candles for the candelabra and enough dishes and bowls in which to serve the food.

Flowers – whatever you prefer

When planning, think of which flowers you would like and how they will be arranged. If you want something special, you should order it from the florist in plenty of time. Take the vase you intend to use to the florist, so they can advise you on what would be suitable, but put forward your own ideas as well. The more experience you have, the more critical you are likely to be of the selection of flowers on offer. Look out for strong healthy foliage and flowers. In many cases you will probably just buy blooms and combine them in a bouquet with fresh greenery from the garden or countryside according to your own taste and preferences.

The professionals – when you want something extra-special

Use the services of professionals who know a thing or two about celebrations and seating plans. Some catering services only offer buffets, others just about anything connected with parties and celebrations. You can hire all the equipment and even waiting staff if you need to. If you want to serve a very refined meal at home, but don't want to slave over a hot stove, you can hire a chef who will prepare the finest delicacies to your personal requirements.

Do you want there to be something more to your celebration than just a meal together? Many entertainers, disc jockeys, musicians, small chamber ensembles, stand-up comedians, magicians and other experts make their services available.

Where can you find these professionals? Through *Yellow Pages*, of course, and in your local telephone directory. Perhaps friends and acquaintances who are experienced hosts can provide you with names and addresses; and restaurants are usually able to put you in touch with the specialists.

The routine – practice makes perfect

A few general tips can help to make your next table decoration more successful.

Don't be afraid to improvise. If you haven't got enough crockery or cutlery for a particular occasion, put different patterns together in such a way that it is cleverly done and looks as though it was what you intended all along. It helps if you do a dry run, without a specific occasion in mind. Simply mix a few different plates, glasses and items of cutlery and see what you think of the effect. You'll then know the best combination to use for the occasion proper.

Be a magpie. If you haven't got many materials for decorations and if you'd like to use the pebbles you picked up on the beach in summer on your table in winter, then it is worth having a little store of items which might one day be used as

decorative ideas to help to realise a table design. You can test whether or not your finds are suitable for this purpose in your own time.

Write things down. If you make a note of all the things you and your family like to eat, if you write down the recipes so you don't forget the details, such as the extra touch which made it

special, then what's wrong with doing the same for decorative ideas? If a table design is a success, why not use it again?

Try things out. If your courage almost fails you at the thought of how perfectly other people turn their hands to such things, then spring into action. Using a wide strip of ribbon, practise tying big decorative bows until you get them right. Make up pretty bouquets using flowers and leaves from the garden. Fold napkins into different shapes. Lay a tablecloth across a table in lots of different ways. Try it. You'll notice how quickly the divide between you and the experts shrinks, and you might have fun experimenting too.

Index

Beate Rabe developed table decoration over many years, first as a serious hobby, then as a part-time job in many fields relating to tables and place settings. Her small agency provides personal advice for event organisers, designs and makes decorations for many occasions, offers introductory courses for anyone interested in the art of table setting and has now produced this illustrated book.

Klaus Arras studied photographic technology at college in Cologne, with emphasis on audio-visual media and picture composition. His previous work has concentrated on still-life photography; more recently he has become increasingly involved with food photography. He has had his own photographic studio in Cologne since 1985 and works primarily for advertising agencies, industry and publishers of cookery books.
Mrs Xenia Burgtorf is responsible for the styling in many of his photographic productions, as is the case with the photographs in this book.

Translated from the German by Karen Green
in association with First Edition Translations Limited, Cambridge, UK
Colour photography: Klaus Arras
Styling: Xenia Burgtorf
Editor: Birgit Rademacker

ACKNOWLEDGEMENT
Special thanks are due to the following, for their invaluable help in the preparation of this book:
Wilhelm Daume GmbH, Bergisch Gladbach
Eins-Zwei-Drei, Norbert Timm GmbH, Cologne
Karin Niessen, Mode und Wohnen, Leverkusen
Pesch GmbH & Co. KG, Furnishings, Cologne
Sticken und Schenken, Kiel
Restaurant Isenburg, Cologne-Holweide
Restaurant Schloß Georgshausen, Hommerich bei Lindlar